THE PERFECT HAIRCUT

LWOKYA EDGAR

DEDICATION

I would like to first of all dedicate this book to the love of my life, my little princess, my daughter, **Edlin.** A diamond in my eyes, she has always been my reason and my fire through all my passions and aspirations. Born while I was still a medical undergraduate, she still inspires hope and meaning into my life. Though the times were rough as we tried to make ends meet, she was and still is that glittering spark in my darkest hours.

And to the ray of sunshine in my life, the pillar of my dream, my soul mate **Mary**. It was in my lowest and darkest moments of my life that she shown her brilliant and beautiful rays upon my soul. Our meeting was something that was orchestrated and planned in a magnificent and immaculate way long before we were even born. It is also to her that I dedicate this book for that extra-ordinary touch of love and support that she showed me even while being unaware of the direction her desires were leading her.

CONTENTS

ACKNOWLEDGMENTS

Images created and edited by author. Every effort has been made to produce an original collection of material. Feel free to contact us at address above in case of any inquiries.

Creation of print **(Title ID: 5824357)** by Creatspace, a DBA of On Demand Publishing, LLC.

BISAC Category: Design and Fashion

Publisher Company: Edlos Empire Investments

Publishing Platform: Kindle Direct Publishing (KDP), Amazon USA, Inc.

Printed and bound by ПП "Аніка-М" Printing. Pekarska 47 Lviv, Ukraine.

DESIGNING COMPANY:

Designed and Detailed by Mary Ann.

Mary Ann Photography (MS).

PREFACE

The Perfect Haircut is a journey of a boy pushing his way to the surface of the deep waters of life's challenges. The book entails a very specific procedure that the Author got to discover out years of experience as a barber. The procedure involves a specific system that allows an ensures the creation of a perfect haircut.

When someone says a perfect haircut, it involves essential basic steps that need to be taken in order to achieve this perfection. This book dares to explain the simplicity to hair cutting while drilling deep into the procedural system of the guidelines.

This book focuses on a basic trend that is easy to master and implement in order to make a perfect haircut. The book demonstrates the three essential components that are applied in the creation of the perfect haircut also while explaining their general application in detail

The Book also gives a few basic need-to-do instructions on becoming a good barber because giving a perfect haircut to a client is just half the job. This book is for Amateur, Aspiring and Professional barbers looking to perfect their craft.

INTRODUCTION

<u>THE PERFECT FADE</u>

The Perfect haircut requires 3 essential components. They include; **A Perfect Fade, A Perfect Lining** and lastly **Perfect machines**.

A fade is that part of a haircut that possesses an incremental smooth transition of hair from the light portions to the dark portions of the hair.

The light portions represent the regions of the haircut with the least amount of hair. The dark portions represent the regions of the haircut with the most amount of hair.

In order to create a perfect fade, the proportions and anatomy of a client's head must be taken into consideration. Fades can be made on any part of the head and therefore the location of the fade is not important. The ability to put fades at different locations on the client head adds flavor and style to the haircut.

There are 10 types of Fades. These include;

1. All Round-Side Fade
2. Tempo Fade
3. Low All Round-Side Fade
4. High All Round-Side Fade
5. Side Burn Fade
6. Moustache Fade
7. Beard Fade
8. Occipital or Neck Burst Fade
9. Picture Fade
10. Written Fade

To create the all round side fades, a specific system of fractions is used. This system is called the **248 Guideline system**.

The creation of the perfect fade is done in 3

stages;

1.The creation of the Guidelines
2.The Removal of the Guidelines
3.The Detailing of the Haircut

STAGE 1

CREATION OF THE GUIDELINES

The 248 Guideline System

The side part of the client's head can be divided into 3 different portions. The purpose of the division of the head into portions is to create a guideline system. The side of client's head is divided into 2 large half portions, 4 medium quarter portions and 8 small third portions.

The 2 Halves

Region A

This is the first half and is called region A. It stretches from the top of the ear to the angle of the eye-line.

Region B

This is the second half and is called region B. It stretches from the angle of the eye-line to the fore-head hairline.

The 4 Quarters

Regions A and B have 2 other quarter portions within each region called divisions A1 and A2

Division A1

This is the first division, A1. It stretches a quarter way upwards of region A starting from the top of the ear.

Division A2

This is the second division, A2. It stretches a quarter way upwards of region A from the end of A1 to the angle of the eye-line.

Division B1

This is the first division, B1. It stretches a quarter way upwards of region B from the angle of the eye-line.

Division B2

This is the Second division, B2. It stretches a quarter way of region B from the end of B1 to the Fore Head hairline.

The 8 Thirds

The 4 divisions, A1;A2 and B1;B2, also have 2 other additional third portions each. They are classified into 2 parts; Closed lever of the machine with or without Teeth (CT) and Open lever of machine with or without teeth (OT). All parts stretch a third way upwards the haircut.

1st Part A1

This is the First part of division A1 called CT0. This means that the machine's lever is placed in the closed position with no tooth or guard.

2nd Part A1

This is the second part of division A1 called OT0. This means that the machine's lever is placed in the open position with no tooth or guard.

1st Part A2

This is the first part of division A2 called CT1. This means that the machine's lever is placed in the closed position with Number 1 tooth or guard attached to it.

2nd Part A2

This is the second part of division A2 called OT1.This means that the machine's lever is placed in the open position with Number 1 tooth or guard attached to it.

1st Part B1

This is the first part of division B1 called CT2. This means that the machine's lever is placed in the closed position with Number 2 tooth or guard attached to it.

2nd Part B1

This is the second part of division B1 called OT2. This means that the machine's lever is placed in the open position with Number 2 tooth or guard attached to it.

1ˢᵗ Part B2

This is the first part of division B2 called CT3. This means that the machine's lever is placed in the closed position with Number 3 tooth or guard attached to it.

2ⁿᵈ Part B2

This is the second part of division B2 called OT3. This means the machine's lever is placed in the open position with Number 3 tooth or guard attached to it.

If both regions A and B are needed the a low all round-side fade is created but if region B is not needed, then a high all round-side fade is created.

STAGE 2

REMOVING THE GUIDELINES

After creating the guidelines with the 248 guideline system, a smooth incremental transition from the light portions to the dark portions of the haircut is created by removal of the guidelines.

The process of removing the guidelines is done by a process called **the Up-C stroking method** of cutting. The machine is gradually opened up from the closed position as the barber moves up the side of the head while adding the appropriate teeth or guards in the right portions and regions of the haircut.

THE 248 GUIDE

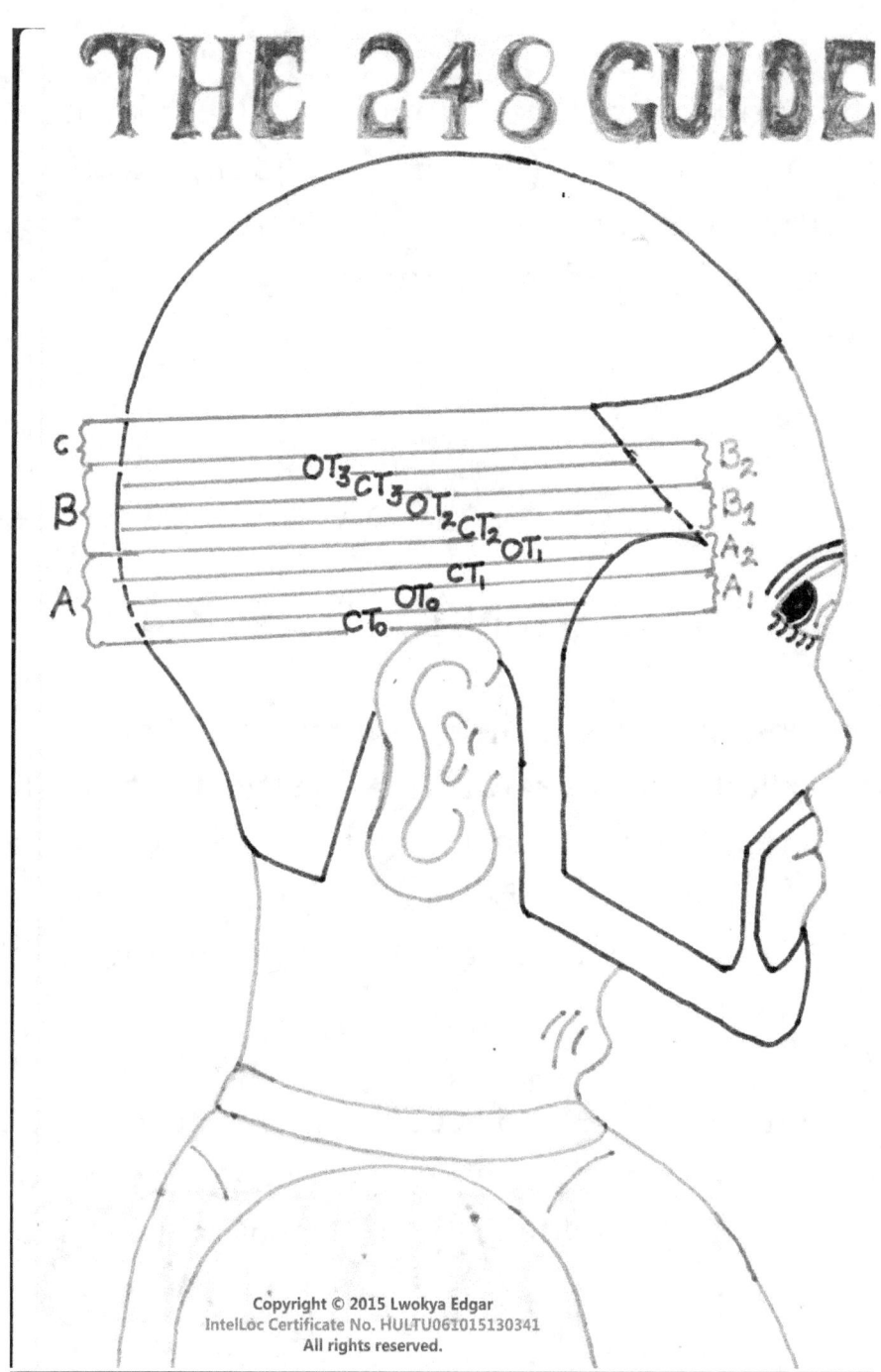

Another method would involve placing the machine on its side and use its tips to remove the guidelines and any hair preventing a smooth blending of the portions created

STAGE 3

DETAILING THE HAIRCUT

This involves using a radical yet easy method called the **Scratching Method** of cutting. This is done by placing the machine (CT0) on its side as the barber scratches through the faded regions to create a smooth well detailed haircut.

The machine is placed on it side to reduce the amount of hair cut as the barber tries to even out the transition by removing uneven dark regions.

PERFECT LINING

This involves the study and analysis of the anatomy and proportions of the client's face because every client has a different face anatomy. In order to make the Perfect lining, an imaginary line needs to be drawn on the clients face.

The Fore Head Hairline (FHL)

An imaginary straight and horizontal line is drawn from a point that is a quarter way of region B at one side of the head to another similar point on the other side of the head.

The Tempo Hairline (TH)

This diagonal hairline is divided into 3 parts; TH1, TH2 and TH3

Tempo Hairline 1 (TH1)

This line runs diagonally from the inner corner of the eye on the opposite side of the head to meet the Fore Head hairline.

Tempo Hairline 2 (TH2)

This line runs diagonally from the Fore Head Hairline to the outer corner of the eye on same side of the head.

Tempo Hairline 3 (TH3)

This line runs diagonally from the Outer corner of the eye to the top of the ear on the same side of the head.

The Side Burn Hairline (SBL)

This line runs straight downwards from the top of the ear to the bottom of the ear.

The Beard Hairline (BL)

This line runs diagonally alone the chin bone from the bottom of the ear to half way the side part of the head

The Moustache Hairline (ML)

This line runs diagonally from the top of the ear to the moustache edge. The moustache is trimmed in a semi circle under the nose.

Once the lines are created, different styles and curves are added along the hairline. It is important to follow the natural hairline and only cut as much as 3 mm into the hairline if needed in order to create a perfect curve of the hairline.

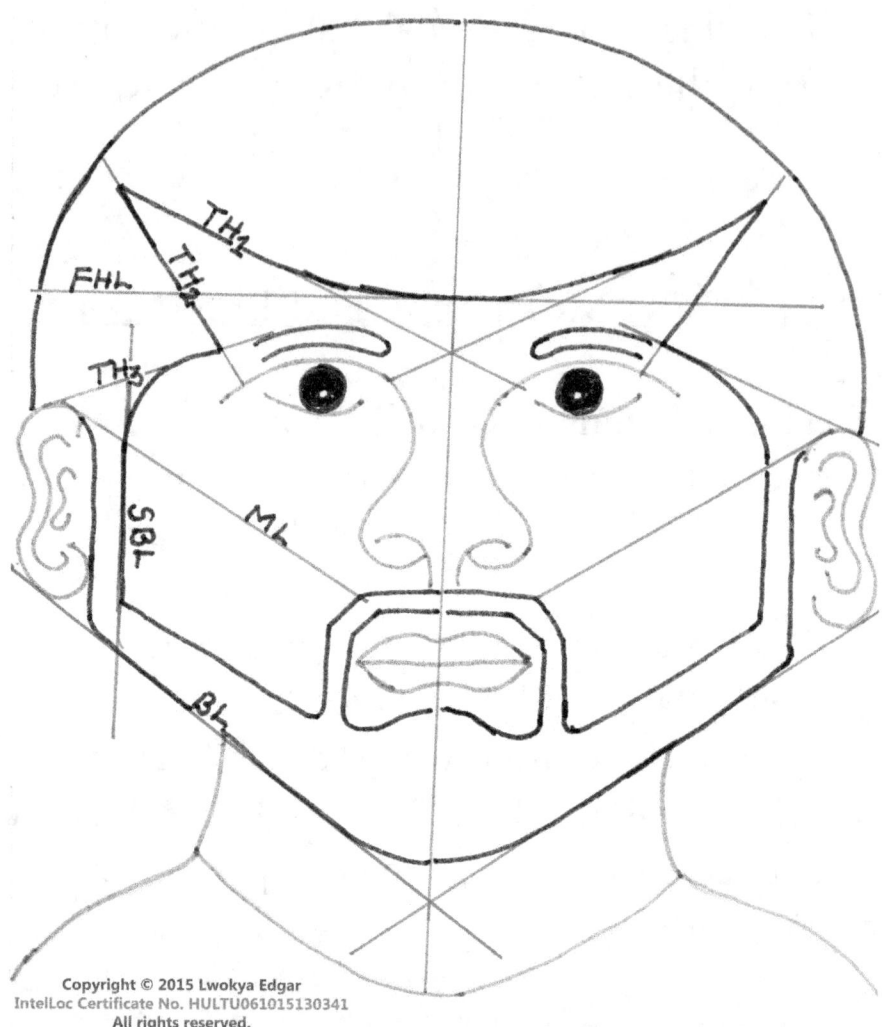

THE HAIRLINES

PERFECT MACHINES

The Perfect machine involves 3 types of equipment;

1. The Perfect Clipper
2. The Complete number of teeth or guards (0mm-12mm)
3. The Perfect Trimmer and Shaver

The Perfect Clipper

The perfect clipper can vary depending on the brand names. There are a few brand names that produce the best clippers. It is from these brands that a perfect clipper can be got. They are;
- Andis Brand
- Wahl Brand
- Phillips Brand
- Rowenta Brand

The Complete Number of Teeth

The complete number of the teeth or guards must be included for the perfect machine equipment to used. The zero tooth number is very important because it removes the line OT0 created by 1st Part A1 (OT0) in order to create the perfect fade.

The Measurements of the Teeth

Region A – OT1 – 6mm

Region B – OT3 – 12mm

Division A1 – OT0 – 3mm

Part CT0 – 0mm

Part OT0 – 1.5mm

Zero Tooth/Guard – 1.5mm

Division A2 – OT1 – 6mm

Part CT1 – 3mm

Part OT1 – 3mm

Division B1 –OT2 – 9mm

Part CT2 – 3mm

Part OT2 – 6mm

Division B2 – OT3 – 12mm

Part CT3 – 6mm

Part OT3 – 9mm

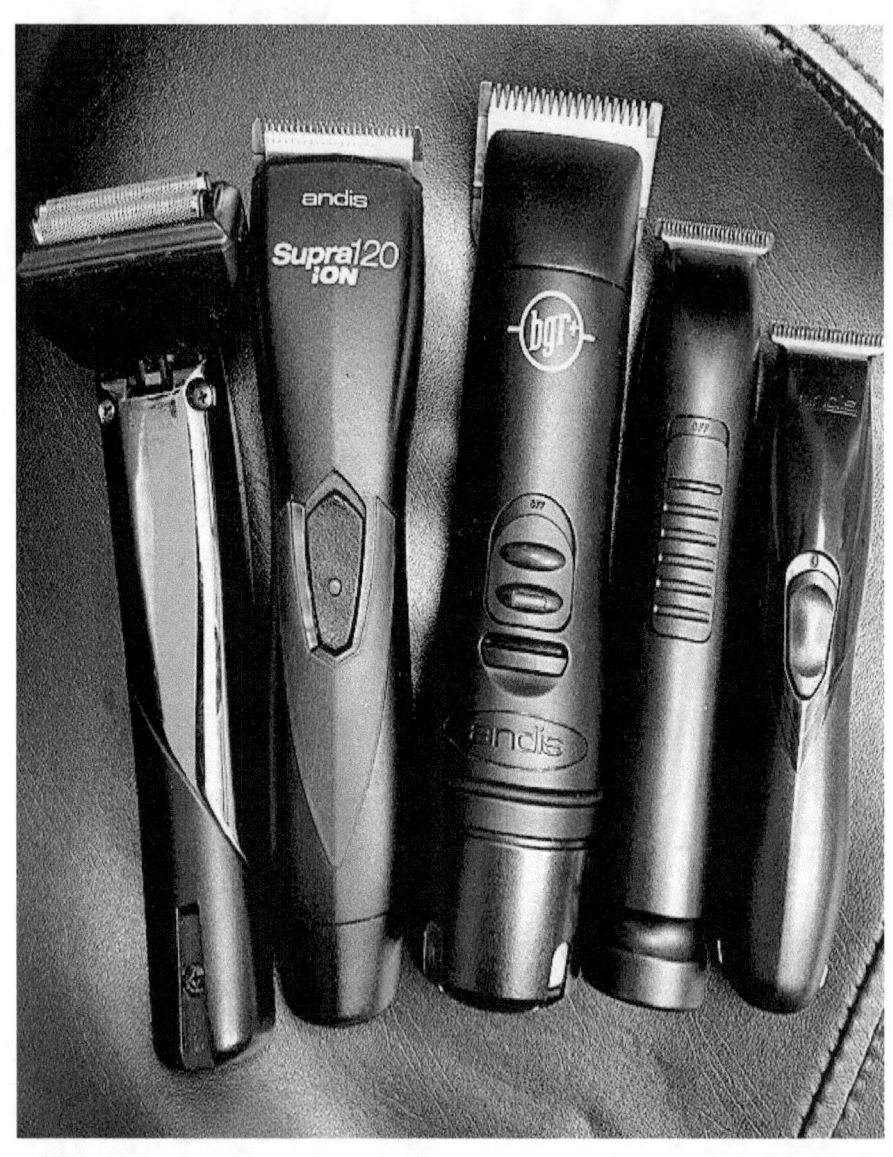

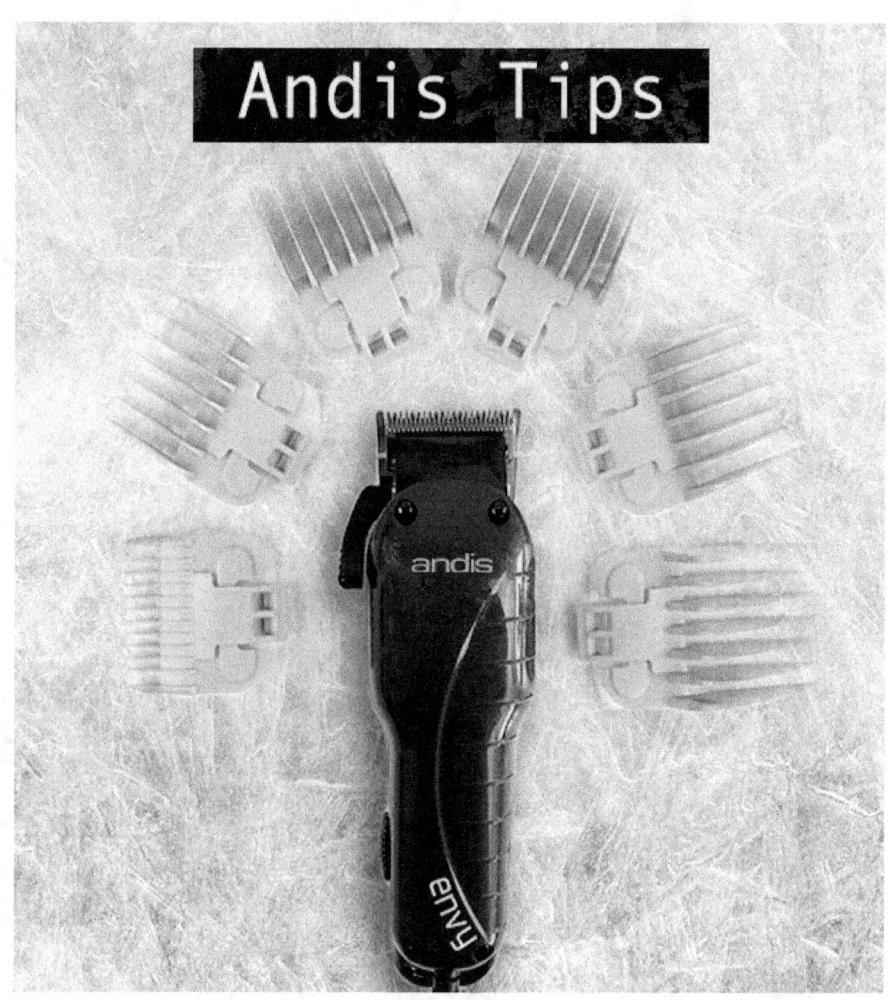

THE PERFECT TRIMMERS/
SHAVERS

This involves the same type of brands as the brand of the clippers. One important reminder is not to always keep your trimmers zero gaped. This can injure the client.

ABOUT THE AUTHOR

I was born on the 16th of September 1986 in the heart of the capital city, Kampala, where I had my earlier education and completed my high school before moving to Ukraine were I firmly established my life. I took an undergraduate study in medicine at a medical state university in Lviv city then later decided to get involved in business in order to create a legacy for myself and for all those who will come after me. This decision lead me to build a company from scratch.

I have always been fascinated about perfection so I guess this book is the reason why it has always been my dream to express my inspiration concerning the haircuts. These concepts developed over many months of research and experience as a barber. I come from a humble background and I have had an interesting life journey which is why I thought I should share my story with the world.

www.ingramcontent.com/pod-product-compliance
Lightning Source LLC
Chambersburg PA
CBHW061937280526
45787CB00004B/1630